LOVE, SEX, AND ROMANCE:

BEAUTIFUL LOVE POEMS FOR THE HEART

Ed Hendricks

Copyright © 2009, 2012 by Edward Hendricks

This is a work of both fiction and non-fiction. Actual persons, places, songs, and events helped inspire me to write this special book. I wish to extend my deepest thanks and respect to all those who are mentioned.

And lastly, this book was formerly titled "Stars, Dreams, and Romance: A Collection of Simple and Beautiful Love Poems." This new version was updated in May 2012. I added 8 new poems in addition to making other changes.

ISBN   0-6156-1130-3

Printed in the United States of America

Table of Contents

Titles with a * are new poems in this updated version.

"I wrote a love poem or two, or three, or four
Inspiration took over, so I wrote many more

Then one day, I took a look
And discovered I had written an entire book

INTRODUCTION

Hello to all the deep hearts in the world, and thank you for taking the time to read this special book of poetry. As you can tell from the title, the main subject is about love.

Love. A four-letter word that means so much and goes so far. In this crazy, hectic, and often confusing world, one may want to believe that love is understood by few and misunderstood by many. Each of us as living, breathing human beings has our own thoughts and ideas about what love is and what love should be

.

This book is *my* thoughts and ideas on love.

In this book of love poems, we shall go to the stars together and we will dream about love together. We will explore those feelings of love, romance and sex, and we will look at other types of love and what caused the feelings behind them.

The style of this book is very simple and plain. I have read (and I am sure you have too) poetry in which I had to sit there and think hard about what the author was trying to say. So I write ALL my poems in a style that is very easy to read and easy to understand. Also, before you read each poem, you will find out my thoughts behind the poem. What I was thinking about or what inspired me to write each of the poems. I feel that in revealing these facts, you will be able to better feel my emotions as I wrote each poem and you will be able to follow my thoughts as to why I wrote the poem.

I thank you again for your time. Now, let this wonderful journey of the heart begin…

DEDICATIONS

This book is dedicated to God, who is love and is the creator of love. I thank you for blessing me with the talent of writing and expressing my thoughts about your great gift to humanity.

To my mother, Ms. Dorothy B., whose inspiration and dedication were priceless. I could not have done this great work without you Mom. Thanks so much for everything.

To Oprah Winfrey, whom I have admired for many years and look up to as a positive influence in my life. At times, I wanted to give up on writing this book, but I remembered that you never quit going for your dreams. Thank you for your persistence.

To radio and television personalities Michael Baisden and Steve Harvey, who took the hard road to publish their books and have encouraged me and millions of listeners and viewers to keep going for our dreams. Thank you both for supporting so many of us dreamers.

To Karina Goncharova, of Kharkiv, Ukraine, who agreed to let her beautiful picture of the two lovers in silhouette appear on the front cover of this book. As soon as I looked at it, I knew I had to have it on the cover. Thank you so very much for such an amazing photo.

To all the musicians who helped to inspire me to do something unusual, and write a poem about certain songs they made. With deep humility and respect, I honor your creativity.

To my cats G-Rock and Asia who sat with me many a night

and day as I was writing this book. I thank you both for your "help." May you both rest in peace.

And lastly, to you, the readers of this book. I wish you all the best of life and in love.

DIFFERENT LOVE POEMS

I would like to start this book with poems, which some are not of a romantic nature, but the feelings behind them still come from and are based on love. There are many types of love and I would like to express my feelings on some of those.

Also, I wish to express my admiration of certain people as well. Their accomplishments were an inspiration to me and I want to show them my appreciation in this section.

Ed Hendricks

OF MOM AND OPRAH

ABOUT THIS POEM:

This poem is about my admiration for two women that have inspired my life and touched it deeply. They are my mother, Ms. Dorothy B., and Oprah Winfrey. The idea for this poem came to me as I was thinking about people who I feel have left a positive influence on my life. In today's world, a lot of people tend to look up to some bad role models as their heroes. So I looked at my heroes and came up with these two wonderful ladies.

Two women whose lives are so separate, yet I see as equals

Oh mother,
Through my eyes I have seen your life unfold
I have witnessed your joys and pains
Your highs and lows, your strengths and weaknesses
I have seen your tears and caused your tears
I have seen those whom you loved wrong you, almost unto your death
Not an easy life you have led
But I still love you
And deeply respect you

Ms. Winfrey,
The eyes of the world have seen your life story
For we know how you rose from humble beginnings
Your successes and failures
Those you have helped and those that hurt you

Love, Sex, And Romance

We have felt your joys, and shared your pains
Yet you have remained strong

An amazing woman worthy of much praise
And like my mother, worthy of the deepest of respect

Oh ladies,
Separate yet equal I see you
Separate yet equal you have lived
Separate in lives, equal in emotion, struggle, and bravery

Through my eyes I have lived with you both
Admired you both
Respected you both
One for the love of son to a devoted mother
One for the love of an outstanding and inspiring human being

You ladies have overcome great odds
The powers of persistence, determination, and prayer were
your allies
In becoming the fantastic women I see you as

You both have captured my heart
Dazzled my imagination
Ignited my inspiration
And enriched my life
Because of the way you have lived yours

My love goes out to you ladies
And may God bless you both

Ed Hendricks

WRITE TO YOUR LOVE

Please use this page to write some words of love to someone special.

ONE GUN

ABOUT THIS POEM:

I want to start out by telling you that I wrote this poem because of my love and compassion for my fellow human beings who were, and are hurt by gun violence. While watching the evening news one night, a story came on in which a 16-year-old boy was shot and killed for no good reason. His mother was on the TV, crying her heart out and asking why this had to happen. My heart went out to her as I felt her pain. I wish I could have reached through the TV and given her a big hug of comfort and reassurance.

To add more to the television part of this, one TV show I like to watch is on the A&E Network titled The First 48,™ in which a homicide has been committed and the detectives try to solve it inside of 48 hours. It is usually a gun that has been used in the crime.

Needless gun violence is totally out of control, and most of it is unnecessary. How many people have died and will die worldwide because of such thoughtless actions? When will it stop?

I could go on and on about this subject, but it is not my intention to lecture. Instead, I will let this poem do all my talking.

Ooooh, the troubles One Gun has caused
Lifetimes of tears, sadness, and sorrows

Mothers, sisters, fathers, brothers
Aunts, nieces, uncles, nephews
Children, teens, adults young and old
Grandmothers, Grandfathers
Have all felt the pain from One Gun

One Gun has no brain
No mind
No personality
No feelings
But the one behind it does

One Gun has no thought
No good sense
No common sense
But the one behind it does

One Gun cannot say, "No, I will not pull this trigger."
One Gun will not say, "There is another way to solve this."
One Gun does not say, "Let's talk my friend, my brother, or even my lover."
But the one behind it can

When One Gun is filled, and then emptied
Lives are emptied
Homes are emptied
Schools are emptied
While the jails and the graveyards are filled

When One Gun speaks
Blood leaks
When you see One Gun's breath
Someone may smell of death

Love, Sex, And Romance

Billions of tears, One Gun has shed
The color of fear, One Gun loves red

Where there are drugs, One Gun is there
When there are hugs, One Gun is rare

Dividing the races, One Gun has caused
Teary-eyed faces, One Gun needs to be paused

Rich or poor, suburb or ghetto
One Gun does not care where the blood flows

All over the Earth
One Gun has been felt
Not a blessing but a curse
One Gun has dealt

At the movies, or at work
One Gun still has gone berserk

Churches, malls, school halls, even city hall
One Gun has touched us all

But One Gun has its limits
The hand that holds it
The mind that controls it

That mind can be educated
To never pick up One Gun
That mind can be re-educated
To put down One Gun

And the hands that hold One Gun

Ed Hendricks

Can shake another hand in peace
And the hands that held One Gun
Can be put together . . .

In prayer

I LOVE MY FREEDOM (THE MASTER AND THE SLAVE)

ABOUT THIS POEM:

This poem is about my twelve years of using drugs (marijuana) and alcohol. Twelve years of my life that I lost due to my own stupidity. I wanted to say here that after finally making the decision to stop using them both, I feel much better about myself and have learned to love myself once again.

On the television program The Judge Mathis Show™, Judge Greg Mathis tells how he started out doing bad things in his youth. But he was given a second chance and he cleaned up his life and went on to become a judge. I feel like I was given another chance as well when I stopped using the two.

I also wish to give this poem to ALL those who have or still are battling the same thing or some other addiction. I hope this poem will inspire you to take back your life as well.

Twelve years
For twelve years, I was not me
For twelve years, I was not free

That which I could have been I was not
That which I could have done I did not
Those whom I could have helped
Received nothing

For I was imprisoned by two masters

And I gave them much help
Masters I helped to create
For I gave them "the key" over me when I gave in to their
poisonous influence
Again and again

Marijuana and much alcohol were my masters' names
Enemies that humanity knows well
Including me

For twelve years I was their willing slave
Masters of comfort I thought they were
When in reality they were creators of my destruction

Those who were "jailed" with me
They looked up with me, served with me
For my masters were theirs too

"No, I am not high" I would say
But those who loved me knew better
"That's not alcohol you smell"
But again, those who loved me knew better

Stupidity was in my left hand
Idiocy was in my right hand
For some of the crazy things I did under my masters' control

At a party serving my masters in December 1991
Driving home very late
"How did I wake up in this field?"
I was lucky I woke up at all

Good sense later told me

Love, Sex, And Romance

Next time, you may not be so lucky
For your luck will soon run out
Common sense told me
Good sense was right

Good sense told me
Your masters are going to kill you, or get you killed
Again, common sense said
Good sense was right

January 1, 1992, a New Year's resolution I made
To escape from my masters' control
A firm decision to stop serving them
And to take back the precious things they took from me: My
mind, my time, and my life

But my body remembered their false feelings of pleasure
It screamed its rebellion nonstop
"Traitor! Coward! You need us! You will always need us!"
But I proved them wrong

Twenty seven+ years later I am still free

No doctor's office for the mind did I visit
No treatment center knew of me
For determination and persistence were my counselors

Instead, I took up running and weights
Building up my body and my mind
Undoing the damage from years of abuse

My masters are now faded memories
Powerless to stop me from releasing my potential

So wonderfully free do I feel
I can touch the sky
I can glide with the clouds
I can soar to the stars
I see the ordinary as a new world

My senses are alive once more because of my freedom

The price I paid for my freedom
In tears, in shame
In sorrow, in lost years, in hurt loved ones
I am determined to never pay again

For I love you all, my family
I love you, my friends
And most importantly

  I love myself

A MOTHER, ABOUT MOTHERS

ABOUT THIS POEM:

To all of humanity, the Earth is the ultimate mother and she has something to "say" about how we should treat our human mothers with the love and respect they are entitled to and deserve.

My children
All my beloved children
As your mother, The Earth
I want to honor the mothers of my children
For without them, your lives would not exist

From his heart God created mothers
Their love is as deep as His

A mother's love is heroic
For there would be no tales of heroes if it were not for them

Nature proves the wisdom of a mother's love
So powerful are the jaws of the mother alligator
But see how she tenderly cares for her young
Does not the mother tiger do the same?
The queen of the air is the mother eagle
See how she protects and shelters her young

A rose in full bloom
Compares to the heart of a woman
And a mother

17

My children
All my wonderful children
Your mothers are my children too
And as I care for them

So should you

The bearers of all life
The caretakers of all families
"When mom is not happy, no one is happy"
Is how the saying goes

When fathers are absent, mothers still care
But just as my father loves and respects me
So too should your fathers love and respect mothers
For there would be no fathers
If it were not for mothers

To my little children and young adults
May you show your mothers the same love and respect
For like fathers too
You would not be here if it were not for mothers

My children
All my adorable children
May you all never forget that I am a mother too
I share your mothers' happiness and sadness
I feel their tears of joy and tears of pain
So what you think of mothers is what you think of me
And how you treat mothers is how you will treat me

I have loved all of you, my children
From the time you were born

Love, Sex, And Romance

And to the day you return back to me
I will love you all, unconditionally
Like your mothers have done
And still are doing

Ed Hendricks

THE STRENGTH OF A WOMAN

ABOUT THIS POEM

The inspiration for this poem came from the song "A Woman's Worth" by Alicia Keys. Women all over the world have made much progress in many areas. In some things, they shine brighter than men. I see this as a sign of inner strength and wisdom and I just want to let ALL the women of the world know my thinking by writing this poem of great respect.

To Man,

I am WOMAN

WOMAN means **WO**rthy of **MAN**

I am MORE THAN worthy of your respect
Your praise, your admiration,
And your love

I may not be stronger than you physically
Emotionally and mentally, I am more than your match
My strength is more inside than outside
For the world sees, feels, and knows my power

You cannot buy what I am worth, but you can earn it
With your respect, praise, admiration
And again, your love

WOMAN means being **W**ith **O**ur **MAN**

Love, Sex, And Romance

I am with you because I WANT TO be with you
For you have EARNED my devotion
By your side I choose to be

NEVER behind you should I walk
Together we are as one
Completing and complementing each other

WOMAN means being **WO**nderfully **M**ade **A**nd **N**urturing

I nurture, I nourish, I protect
The wonder of creation lies within me
I was beautifully made for this purpose
And for many others, as you have already read about

You have trusted me to raise our children
Teach them, discipline them
Love them

For what I do for our children
I do for you as well

WOMAN means **W**isdom **O**f **M**any **A**ges **N**ow

I am wise in my own ways
Mostly different, sometimes the same as yours

Through the ages, my wisdom has been proven
Curie, Mother Teresa, Thatcher, and many others
Are the inspiring foremothers of today's women

Wisdom and nature always are one
Wisdom is also one of my natural abilities

I am WOMAN

I am **WO**rthy of **MA**g**N**ificence

And my strength

WOrks for the good of hu**MAN**ity

Special Note: I also would like to give a big shout out to the song "Respect" by Aretha Franklin. That song is the anthem for women all over the world to be treated with the respect and dignity they deserve. Even though it was recorded in the 60s, its message still holds true today. Thank you so very much Ms. Franklin! May you rest in peace.

MY BRAVE FACE (Malala Yousafazi)

ABOUT THIS POEM

In the last poem, "The Strength of a Woman," I gave honor to the strength and wisdom of women all over the world. This poem is about one extraordinary young lady. The Taliban in Afghanistan shot Malala Yousafzai in the head and she survived. She now is a Nobel Prize winner who encourages and inspires girls and women worldwide. Her amazing story inspired me to write this poem about her.

This face that the world looks upon
Represents the faith of a nation
The hope of millions
For the promise of a better future

My eyes are focused on the goal of change
For my country
And for humanity

My nose has smelled overwhelming fear
And terrible death

Now my mouth speaks for the blameless
And the innocent

The innocent whose souls cry out to heaven for justice
And hope for a brighter future

The heartbeat of a nation is its people's knowledge

Ed Hendricks

Shared knowledge which leads to progress
My heart beats with those that want change

Those who see change as necessary
To move forward to greatness

Ignorance has turned beauty into courage
Injustice, the result of that ignorance, has changed this
ordinary face
Into one filled with dreams, determination

My brave face bears the scars of senseless violence
But it has survived to become a face of inspiration

Does God love more the faces of those who kill in his name?
Or does he truly love the brave faces of the faultless?

This faith I have in God, that he cherishes the innocent
Fuels my desire, ignites my soul
Inspires my imagination to believe that anything is possible

Today my noble face survives
To imagine, to dream, to yearn
To uplift those being persecuted for wanting a better life

Will my brave face inspire yours to speak out against the evils
being done worldwide?

May my brave face join with many other brave faces
To show all that ONE brave face can make a difference

Love, Sex, And Romance

LOVE EACH OTHER (THE STUPIDITY OF RACISM)

ABOUT THIS POEM

In this poem I wanted to tell how dumb racism in all its forms is. Racism has divided humanity among so many lines, and when and where it divides, it has conquered. Racism is the root cause behind some of history's great wars. (The American Civil War and World War II come to mind.) And once again, the Earth has to endure this plague upon her lands.

My children,
All my darling children
Please pay heed to the words of one of my children
For some of the reasons why you dislike one another
Make no sense to me
And this has caused both you and me
Great pain, suffering and much death
Please my children do this for me

My brother and my sister
Outside, I may not look like you
But inside, I am just like you
Our hearts beat, our blood is red
Our lungs breathe, we live and we love

So why can't we love each other as brothers?
As sisters? As another human being?
Why must we let differences in color
In race
In religion

In politics
In money
In where we live
In where we are from
In work
In clothes
In cars
And so much more separate us?

I look at you and I see my human brother
My human sister
My human neighbor
My human friend

Are we not all sharing one beautiful planet?
One planet with different parts all working together
So as the Earth sets the example of working together as one
Why can't we as humans do the same?

The Earth moves and exists in wisdom
For wisdom and nature move as one
But racism exposes the stupidity of humanity
It is taught
It is learned
It is read
It is spoken
It is then unleashed
With dire, and even fatal results

Racism divides, then conquers
It lives and then it kills
The destroyer of dreams
The slayer of hopes

Love, Sex, And Romance

The murderer of justice

My brothers and sisters all over the world
I plead to you to open your heart and minds

To your brothers and sisters who are not like you outside
But inside are the same as you

Open your hand to another as a friend
Again, as a fellow human being who deserves dignity
For when racism goes then love flows

Judge not by the outer, but what the inner character is
Like Dr. King dreamed
And maybe one day his dream will be all of ours

Thank you my brother, my sister

My friend

Ed Hendricks

TWO DIFFERENT PEOPLE, ONE SAME LOVE

ABOUT THIS POEM:

I was listening to the song "Our Love" by Natalie Cole (May she rest in peace) when the inspiration for this poem came to me. In this poem, I wanted to show that no matter what the differences people have, they still could fall in love with each other. There is so much that separates us in this world, but love can overcome them all.

My love,
So what if your skin color is not like mine
That your culture, religion, money, and your past are also not the same
I still love you

For inside your heart and your mind
Is something beautiful the world cannot see
But I have not only seen and felt it
But have fallen in love with

I care not about what you wear outside
For inside you are clothed as my knight in love's armor
I care not where you live outside
For I know your love for me lives inside you

Small minds say because we are so different
We should not fall in love
"Stick to your own kind" they say
But you are my kind

Love, Sex, And Romance

Thoughtful, respectful, loyal, playful, affectionate
And so much more
You are the kind of person I need to make me happy
To make me smile
To light up my eyes
And my heart

In nature, all colors live together
To form beauty and wonder
The sea holds many kinds of life
A garden has plants and flowers of many colors
No two stars are alike
But their shine lights up the darkness

My lover,
We have become one despite our differences
Living and loving forever is our destiny
May our love set an example for those who fall in love with one
who is opposite

Let us prove to the small minds
That we can love just as deep as they can
That we can love just as strong as they can
Maybe our love will open closed minds to the fact
That we are all human inside
No matter what is outside

Ed Hendricks

THE LOVE OF A LIFETIME HAS GIVEN ME A LIFETIME OF LOVE

ABOUT THIS POEM:

I want to honor those who have been married for 30, 40, 50 years or more, with this poem. One of the hardest things in life is to be married for a lifetime. I think very highly of those couples who have stayed in love for years, and I wish them the best of love for the rest of their lives. I also wrote this poem from a man's point of view who has been in love with his wife all these years. This I feel is one of the greatest honors he can give her.

Decades ago we met, and fell in love
Time has flown by so fast
The kids have come and gone
"Grandma and Grandpa" the grandkids call us
Now it is just you and me

A lifetime of love you have given me
But it still seems like yesterday that I fell in love with you

Early in my life, I searched through the void for you
That vast, ever changing chasm of life
Persistence and prayer were on my side
In capturing your love

And as we lived and we loved through the years
I fell in love with you over and over and over again
My beautiful bride

Love, Sex, And Romance

My lovely wife
My loving mother
My exciting lover

Life was not easy for us
Staying in love has had its challenges
We have had our disagreements
The sun has shined on our love
The rain has fallen on our love
But through it all, we still are . . . in love

And now as we are in our golden years
And our bodies have become old
Though my vision is fading
My eyes still light up when they look into yours
The hands of this man are not as steady
But they hold firm when you take my hand

My Eternal Princess,
You have given me your heart
You have shared with me your heart and your soul
So blessed have I been for your lifetime of love
I now know for sure that you are the love of my lifetime
And may I take this wonderful feeling with me
When I go to meet God

Ed Hendricks

THE LADY AND THE PIANO

ABOUT THIS POEM

The idea for this poem came from two places. The first being the singer Alicia Keys. (Again!) After watching a video of her playing the piano as she was singing, I wondered if I could write a poem about her as she played. But no words came to mind. However, I knew my subconscious would give me something sooner or later.

Sometime later, I was watching a rerun of the TV show "Cheaters®" one afternoon. The story was about a lady from Poland (she could have been Russian, but I am not sure) who was being cheated on by her boyfriend. She just happened to be a piano player. As she was telling her story, the camera cut away to another scene in which she was playing the piano. That scene caught my eye for she looked so elegant and so passionate as she played. I then thought about when I watched Alicia Keys play also and suddenly my subconscious kicked into high gear and gave me the words I was at a loss for earlier. Words that you will soon read.

Gazing in adoration at…
A woman so pretty
A lady so beautiful
A vision so splendid
As she plays the piano

My heart fills with delight
My ears are filled with sweet music

Love, Sex, And Romance

My imagination is so mesmerized

Look as her fingers glide with little effort
Across the keys so gracefully they dance
So light, yet so firm is her touch

I wonder what her thoughts are as she plays?
Thoughts of a touch so tender that she wants?
Thoughts of a kiss so deep that she desires?

Her body sways gently with the rhythm
A smooth motion caused by her lovely sound

I watch her in total fascination
In admiration of her skill
In awe of her spirit

Bach, Beethoven, Mozart
In the footsteps of the great ones she now follows
For she plays with their same passion

But she loves with even more passion
For she plays the way she loves
With confidence, with romance
For what is in her heart comes out fully

Dreamy lady,
Your love of the piano is so special, so unique
You have filled many lives with joy and with inspiration

May I speak for all who adore you
And say "thank you so very much"

Ed Hendricks

THE HEART TO WIN

ABOUT THIS POEM:

After watching Michael Phelps win gold medal number eight at the 2008 Summer Olympics, the thought came to mind to write a poem about what he and all the athletes went through to reach their peak. More inspiration for this poem came from Dara Torres, Usain Bolt, Bryan Clay, the USA Men's and Women's Basketball teams, the USA Women's Soccer team, and the Women's Marathon winner, Constantina Tomescu from Romania. These were the achievements that inspired me the most.

But this poem is not only for those who are in sports. This goes out to ALL who have strived to achieve a goal in life, ALL who have reached for their dreams, ALL who have had to overcome great odds to succeed.

"Conceive it, Believe it, Achieve it" is what they say
The challenge to be great, to do great things
Is the challenge life issues all

"Where there's a will, there's a way"
I have the will to win
And the way before me has been set

But the way has been so hard
The road to glory so long
Filled with pain, disappointments, confusion
My frustrations have been many

Countless nights filled with tears
Followed by days of worry
"Should I stay the course?"

"Can I do this?"
"Why am I doing this?"
"Dare I attempt to achieve the impossible?"
So many questions, but few answers

My body bears the scars from the trials
Disciplined to its limits and beyond
So too was my mind
Pushed in ways I never thought possible
Stretched in ways I never dreamed of

How badly I wanted to give up
Many times I wanted to quit
"A quitter never wins" is the saying
So I kept my eye on the prize

"You can't do it"
"Give up now and settle for what you have"
"You will always be a ____ . Just be that"
Deep inside I knew I was better

Their unkind words fueled my determination
To be more, to do more
For they try nothing and always succeed
I choose to dare much
And stand a chance to win

I first saw failure as an enemy
And then later it became a friend

For a true friend teaches you lessons
Sometimes in the hardest way
But you have to leave some "friends" behind
And make new ones
Her name is Victory
His name is Success

For I have fought the fight of my life
Fear and doubt I always battled
Facing the danger of losing much
With courage beyond what is normal

The forces of Hell stood against me
Opposed to my majestic purpose
But faith and persistence sustained me
Determination helped to motivate me
And God had mercy on my magnificent quest

Even in my darkest hour I knew there was a light
Now that light shines so bright on this great day

For my daring has paid off
All the years of hardship, of failures, are memories of the past
Success is now mine

I stand atop this magnificent pinnacle
Having realized the potential within
So wonderful of a feeling
So marvelous of an emotion
To have won at a goal in life

As excitement runs through my body
Knowing I faced overwhelming odds bravely

Knowing I overcame the insurmountable fortress of defeat
And won

And now, when I walk in the glory of the sun
I will hold my head high with a smile
And raise my hands to God
In eternal thanks

INTERLUDE: THE EYES OF LOVE

You know, people say that the eyes are the windows to the soul. And when you look into someone's eyes, you are looking into their soul. Their core. Their very being.

When you gaze into the eyes of someone you love, you want to see the depth of their love for you. To see that glow, that shine which is special made for you. And when you see that special light in their eyes, you know that person loves you and is in love with you.

But the eyes of love are different than "everyday" eyes. The eyes of love have such a splendid glow in them that almost anyone that looks in them can see it.

Everyone's eyes tell a story, good or bad. With love, the eyes can tell a wonderful story for the ages.

My wish for all of you readers is for love to light up not only your eyes, but your hearts and spirits as well.

INSIDE HER EYES

ABOUT THIS POEM:

This poem is the first in a series of three about eyes and love. What I see, feel, and imagine when I look into the eyes of someone I am in love with. I feel the eyes of love are limitless and as you read these three poems, I hope you see and feel the same.

As I look into her lovely eyes

I visualize…

The dawn subsides
The sun arise
A new day begins
With my lover, my best friend

For each and every day
Brings forth a new way
To find out the whats and the whys
Of so much love to see inside your questioning eyes

As I stare into her beautiful eyes

I see…

The ocean, so deep, so wide
The eternal flowing tide
The sea, shining so bright

Ed Hendricks

The longer I stare my heart takes flight

 For through my imagination my heart has found its wings
This is what looking through your eyes brings
How blessed I am to be so close to you
And those eyes that light up so true

Again, when I look into her glowing eyes

My mind pictures...

Nightfall, and all its stars
Some so near, some so far
And the full moon aglow
The Lord has created a divine celestial show

As God is my witness
How can I be so blessed like this
When I behold such marvelous sights
Inside your eyes tonight

As I gaze deeply into her eyes

And fantasize

I imagine...

Stars collide
Galaxies divide
Universes born anew
God's creating is not through

I can imagine the wonders of space

Reflecting through those loving eyes on your tender face
And from distances great and far, through space and time
Before me now two stars brightly shine

And now I am mesmerized

Entranced

Bedazzled

As I lovingly, longingly gaze into her eyes

I FEEL...

Two hearts combine
Our souls entwine
Now we are as one
Tonight love has won

But of all these many splendors
Inside your eyes I see
The most important of all
Is your love for me

EYES OF FOREVER

ABOUT THIS POEM:

Continuing with the theme of the eyes and love, we now come to the second poem in this series. In this poem I will introduce the concept of time and love. (Later on in this book, you will read other poems about this concept)

Also I want to say that this poem is somewhat religious in nature. I based this poem on the Bible verses at Revelation 21:1-4.

Right here, right now
I gaze into your eyes
The love that I see
Devotion that I feel

A thousand years from now
Love still shows in your eyes
Decades have passed
But our love has blossomed

Ten thousand years ahead
It's love that I still see inside your eyes
Time has changed so many things
But again our love has stayed the course

One hundred thousand years have passed
The love in your eyes is ever so bright
Millenniums have come and gone

Love, Sex, And Romance

But my love for you has still grown stronger

So much time has passed
Myriads of years, ages of centuries
And The Lord has blessed us

With his love and with our love
As The Ancient of Days he is timeless, boundless
He is time itself

But my love for you has grown deeper
I look forward to forever loving you
Being in love with you
Falling over and over and over again deeply
Every time I look into your eyes

We now stand at forever
As I gaze into your pretty eyes
Love still shines

Eons of time has gone by
Stars have died out
Galaxies have formed to become universes
Moving through time, space, and beyond
Worlds have been born anew

Earth has become the promised paradise
For the love of God is everywhere
And his love has been with us all this time
And now as forever embraces us
We realize and know
That our love was meant to be
    Forever

NOTE: Some of the subject of this poem will be mentioned in my second book "Knights of Brave Love: The Courageous Quest for Her Eternal Heart."

WHEN GOD LOOKS DOWN

ABOUT THIS POEM:

This poem is the last in the series of eyes and love. I tried to imagine what God sees when he looks down on two people who are in love.

When God looks down, he sees...
The love we feel for each other
How we love each other
The many ways we make love to each other*
All the things we do for each other that say
I love you

When God gazes down upon us, he feels
Our love for him
The love between us, which glorifies him
The love we have for our neighbor

For our love makes God's heart glad
Our love lights up his eyes in delight
"Look and see how they love each other" he says to the angels
As he looks down through the stars

Oh, how great and marvelous he is
The God of total love
Because of his creating, we exist in love
His very being is all of love
With his all-seeing, beaming eyes
Eyes that is 10,000 times brighter than the sun itself

Ed Hendricks

Eyes that can see the thoughts of man
Eyes that can see and feel my love for you

When God looks down, he knows

How much I love you
How much I adore you
The honor and respect I have for you

For when all these things are in his sights
  He smiles at us

* A reference to the poem "Making Love To Her" on page 99.

THOSE EYES

ABOUT THIS POEM:

I was listening to the song "These Eyes" by The Guess Who
and even though it is a sad love song, I thought, "I wonder if I
could turn it into a good love poem." This poem is the result of
that thinking.

When I look into those stunning eyes
My ageless princess
My imagination goes beyond its limits
Past the Earth
And to the stars

For those eyes have stroked my heart
Touched my soul
And caressed my spirit

I see the sun rise inside those open eyes
And feel it set when you close them

A warm summer day turns hot
When I stare into those eyes

A starry night is made brighter
When you gaze up at the stars

I can imagine the ocean
I can dream of the sea
I can picture a gentle flowing stream

Ed Hendricks

Inside those sparkling eyes

Oh Lord, thank you for blessing me
For by your loving spirit

Those eyes are now in love with

My eyes

INTERLUDE: LOVE AND NATURE

A flower so pretty. A sunset so beautiful. The calming, soothing qualities of water. These and so much more are part of nature. Nature has inspired great artists, writers, musicians, and yes, even we poets to reach deep into our hearts and minds and create some of the most eloquent and splendid works the world has ever seen, read, or heard.

What is it about nature that brings out the best of inspiration creativity, and imagination? Maybe it is because nature itself is so marvelous that it touches the hearts of all those who appreciate it and want to express their love for it by having it inspire them to use their talents and abilities. (Wow, that's deep!)

But when nature and love combine, the result is beauty. Pure and natural beauty. I cannot describe it any other way.

In the following poems, you will see how nature inspired me to praise its creator, to praise nature itself, and to magnify both with love.

COMPARISON

ABOUT THIS POEM:

The inspiration for this poem came to me from my mother. She has this rose "garden" in her front yard that "blooms" very few roses. One day I was working with her in her "garden" and the thought occurred to me to compare the heart of a woman to a rose. And this poem is the result of that thinking.

As I gaze at the rose in the early morning sun
I think of her, my one true love

When the morning sunbeams tenderly caress the rose
Reflecting its deep scarlet hue
My mind is joyfully alive
With warm glowing thoughts of her

For is not a rose
Nature's revealed image of a woman's heart
With each petal tenderly placed
Ever so delicately layered
Nestled very snugly
Then encircled in a wondrous natural bosom

And her loving heart, like the glorious rose
In the splendid morning sun
Is an imaginative comparison
To heaven itself

The rose, her heart

Love, Sex, And Romance

When both are touched with love
One is truly blessed

Ed Hendricks

TO GIVE TO YOU

ABOUT THIS POEM:

I wanted to take some of my most favorite things about nature
and turn them into a poem. I hope you all like what I tried to do
here.

 If I could…

I would take the petals from a rose so red
The tint of the ocean, so deep and blue
A ray from the sun, bright and yellow
Wrap them all in my love, and give it to you

I would gather the colors from the elusive rainbow
Some drops of moisture from the early morning dew
The pleasant sounds of a soft summer rain
Bundle them with my love, and give it to you

I would take a beam from the full moon so bright
The glow from a thousand stars born anew
A tender moment of two, from space and time
Group them with so much love, and give it to you

The devotion of two lovebirds, snuggled so close
The passion of two lovers alone together
Honor, respect, adoration in our hearts so true
How I would love to give to you love, forever

UNDER THE WONDER

ABOUT THIS POEM:

Continuing with the theme of some more of my favorite things that I like about nature, I combined them with love, and wrote about them here in another poem.

Also, another source of inspiration for this poem came from the song "Camano Island" by Tony Gable and 206. It is one of the most beautiful instrumental songs I have ever heard and I played this song a lot as I was writing this poem. The song takes you to a place where you want to be with nature and the one you love.

If you go to Youtube.com and type "Tony Gable and 206" in the Search box, "Camano Island" should come up in the search results and you can then hear this amazingly splendid song.

Under the wonder of the early morning sun
Another day of loving you has begun

The start of a new day, and
the splendor of the morning sun
Compares to being in love with you
For every day brings forth
New thoughts, new ideas, new emotions
For life and for love

Under the wonder of a warm summer afternoon

Ed Hendricks

Now our love is in full bloom

A light breeze blows through the trees
And the flowers of the summer have blossomed so pretty
We enjoy the warmth of this beautiful summer day together
The feelings of love between us grows even stronger
And hotter

Under the wonder of a full moon night
Being in love with you feels so right

The moon glows so natural, its glory for all to see
For loving you and being loved by you
Comes so easy and feels so pure
You and the moon with me here tonight
Love has come full circle

Under the wonder of a star filled sky
Falling deeper in love when I gaze into your eyes

As the starry hosts of the heavens
Radiate so magnificently
And the universe displays its majesty
Our love shines with the stars tonight
For just as the stars are one with the night
So too, are we as one with them
And with love

My dear, it's such a lovely sensation
Loving you under the wonders of creation

EXOTICA, ROMANTICA

ABOUT THIS POEM:

Another one of my most favorite jazz songs is "Exotica" by the jazz saxophone musician Paul Taylor. It is an upbeat, catchy tune that reminds me of an adventure on a beautiful island. And to be there with someone you love is truly an adventure of the heart.

And you can also find this song on *Youtube.com* by typing in "Exotica Paul Taylor" in the Search box. This song should come up in the results.

In love with you on an island so tropical
On a day so warm and beautiful
With a breeze so wonderful

Walking on a beach in the sand
Heart-to-heart, hand-in-hand

Stopping to stare at a sea so clear
Admiring its splendor with the one I hold dear

Thinking of how deep its waters are
Knowing our love goes deeper, by far

Come my love; let's walk some more
For us this paradise has so much in store

Gazing at lush plants and trees so exotic

Ed Hendricks

Captivating our eyes for they are enticing and hypnotic

As the sun rises higher
And the day grows warmer
Our love gets hotter

Our senses now awakened as we revel in delight
In awe of all the dreamy sights

Look over there! A small forest with trees
Over to them we stroll, with hearts lighter than a breeze

Into the forest we start to explore
A new little adventure with the one I adore

The sounds of the insects and the birds
I turn and look into your eyes and they need no words

As bodies touch and lips meet
So sweet you taste, such a tender treat

In a place so lovely
Two hearts now so happy
Join as one so joyfully

Exotica

Romantica

ON A SUMMER'S DAY

ABOUT THIS POEM:

Summer is my most favorite time of the year. I love the warmth of the sun on my skin and to feel its light breezes. So I feel like I HAD TO write a love poem about being in love on a summer's day.

On a summer's day

I look into your eyes and say....

 I Love You

On a day so warm with a gentle flowing breeze
A cool wind softly blows through the trees

Pieces of clouds float by against a sky so blue
As I spend a splendid summer's day with you

Strolling through a crowded park hand-in-hand
Sharing a cold drink with you by the ice cream stand

Enjoying the moments, watching people go by
Living the beauty of a summer's day in their eyes

Off on our own, let's find a private place
So I can gaze into those lovely eyes on your face

And say....

I Love You

A secret spot now found under a tall leafy tree
Spreading out a blanket for only you and me

Stretched out on the blanket in the cool grass
Wrapped around each other watching a summer's day pass

Looking at the butterflies floating in the air
Laughing at the squirrels running here and there

Breathing in deep the warm summer air
As I run my fingers through your hair

Special moments like this on a summer's day
Gives me so many more reasons to say...

I Love You

Being with you on a lazy summer afternoon
Not wanting to go anywhere else too soon

Enjoying these moments on a day so fine
Love glowing in our hearts like today's sunshine

We will always remember this time spent together
Lasting memories of this day's summer pleasure

As the setting sun brings this beautiful day to an end
Anticipation asks: "When can we do this again?"

For on another glorious summer's day like this
I will be sure not to miss

Love, Sex, And Romance

The chance to say....

I Love You

Ed Hendricks

A WARM SUMMER NIGHT

ABOUT THIS POEM:

I was listening to the song "Warm Summer Night" by Chic. (Yes, *that* Chic. The disco group from the 70s and 80s. And one of my most favorite bands from that era) and it inspired me to write this poem. The song itself is a deep, breathy and whispery song in which a lady wants more than love on a warm summer night.

I also wanted to take the same feelings of love from "On a Summer's Day" into this night.

On a warm summer night
When love feels so right

In love with you on a warm summer's day
Knowing that feeling tonight will stay

When the stars come out from the sky above
Makes this a perfect night to be in love

Again, let's go to that private place we call our own
Where we can be under the stars alone

Now at that special place, just the two of us
I gaze into your eyes and my heart starts to rush

Your eyes now have that familiar glow
A look that turns a trickle of love into a flow

Love, Sex, And Romance

A stroke of your hair, a touch of your face
A kiss from you makes my heart race

For this warm summer night is suddenly now hot
Your kisses have "hit the spot"

The stars above give off their fire
We start our own with the power of desire

The feel of your body, the taste of your skin
Loves sensual dance now begins

Passion heats up more a summer night so warm
And two bodies move as one in form

Ecstasy explodes into this summer night so beautiful
We know this was much more than physical

Holding each other close and feeling very fine
As the stars above us continue to shine

What an unforgettable warm summer night
In love with you has made it feel so right

SOFT RAIN, GENTLE LOVE

ABOUT THIS POEM:

I love a soft summer rain. And to be in love and take some time out for romance on a rainy day is one of life's true pleasures.

On a lazy summer afternoon
A soft rain begins
The eyes of heaven slowly releases their tears upon the earth

I see that dream-like look in your eyes
That look of hidden desire
My imagination is aroused with visions of romance to come

Inside of an open screened door
You draw me close to you
A soulful kiss follows a tender touch
Another kiss, another touch
And another
And another

Arms around each other we now are
Living in this blissful moment
Enjoying this sweet time alone together

The sound of the slow falling rain
Adds so much more to the affection
Our senses are filled with elation
No words are needed

Love, Sex, And Romance

Now we slowly drift away on this magical day

Two hearts now beat as one
In tune with the rain

Two minds unite in a state of happiness
With the soft rain

And with love.

Ed Hendricks

THUNDERSTORM LOVE

ABOUT THIS POEM:

One Sunday morning, I was awakened by the sound of
thunder and rain. I could not go back to sleep and I lay there
thinking about a past love and what happened between us one
stormy Sunday morning. Inspiration and motivation then took
over and told me I HAD TO get up and write some lines on this
subject.

Sleeping in late on a Sunday morning
Awakened by a crashing sound outside, for now it's storming

And the rain, hard coming down
Sounds like tiny drums hitting the ground

"Good morning honey, how was your sleep?"
"I slept so good, for it was restful and deep"

A quick trip to the restroom, then back to rest
To snuggle more with the one I love best

Holding each other close while listening to the storm
When other feelings of love are born

For suddenly your hands have become more active
I do not resist and into your will I give

The taste of your skin, the feel of your lips
The beats of my heart start to skip

Love, Sex, And Romance

And as love turns to pure desire
Rain and thunder adds to this special fire

Now two bodies move as one in time
Making love on a day without the sunshine

The sounds of passion mixed with the rain
Grows the fire into a roaring flame

When ecstasy's highest point is reached
Thunder lets us know that it too, has peaked

Enjoying the feeling after an experience so great
We catch our breath in this blissful state

Still the storm rages on above
We drift back to sleep, content in love

Ed Hendricks

SEA OF LOVE

ABOUT THIS POEM:

I have always wanted to write a poem about the sea for it has inspired so many people in so many ways. So I mixed the power of love with this thinking, and came up with this little poem.

When I look into the shining sea
And wonder about its deepness
It's calming, soothing nature
My mind thinks so much of…
   You

So beautiful is the sea
The ever-flowing tide
And when the rays of the sun dances on its surface
Memories come up of when I see your eyes light up
In joy and in love

But the depths of the sea cannot hold
The love I feel for you
For my love goes deeper than its fathoms
And wider than it shores

My lovely mermaid of the earth
When you gaze into its crystal waters
And dream about living and loving
Will you fondly think of us?
Will those memories make your heart smile?

Think about the vast reaches of infinity
How wide is eternity
How great God can be
Then think about…
   Me

INTERLUDE: THE STARS AND LOVE

I want to continue the "Love and Nature" theme here in this section. But I want to take it to its highest level. And that level is to take it to the stars.

When I was a child, I remember looking up into the sky at night, and seeing countless numbers of stars. I remember thinking about how pretty they looked and how I wish I could go to them.

Fast forward to my life today and now I see how man has invented space vehicles that can take us closer to the stars than we have ever been. We have even sent different types of vehicles to other planets to explore them, and maybe one day in the future we will actually go to a star.

Even in everyday life as we use the term stars. Movie stars, athletic stars, political stars, and music stars are examples of this. And let us not forget one of the most important events in human history that a star first revealed when it happened: The birth of Jesus Christ.

But to me, it is through the power of love when the stars really shine brightest. It is through the power of love where those stars in our souls shine through our heart. The whole world can see the starlight of the heart of a person who is in love. There is a special glow that such a person gives off and everyone who meets that person can see it.

In some of my poetry, I tried to express those points and to also stretch my imagination to include space, time, the universe, and infinity along with the power of love. Do not lovers want to have many a night together outside under the stars? Is not a starry night one of the most romantic things two people in love can share?

I may not physically ever take that long trip to the stars, but through my imagination and the power of love I can go to the stars. And by sharing these special poems with the world, you can join me. Just make sure you bring the one you love along.

Thank you for letting me share my "star" thoughts with you. And I invite you all to keep on letting those "star lights" in your hearts shine as well.

YOUR SIDE OF THE STARS

ABOUT THIS POEM:

Gazing up at the stars on a warm summer night, I started to think about being in love with someone in another part of the world. This poem is the result of those thoughts. To let her know that I am thinking of her in the warmest way.

Another source of inspiration for this poem came from the song "Somewhere in the World" by one of my most favorite music bands, Swing Out Sister. When I first started writing this poem, I became stuck and put it away until I could think of the right words to finish it. A few days later, I heard this song and words came to me that I felt would work in this poem.

And lastly, I want to "give" this poem to all who have a loved one that they are separated from. Especially those who are away at war. (Iraq and Afghanistan come to mind.) True love has no distance. It is limitless.

Gazing up into the night of a star filled sky
Visions of you are in my mind's eye

For your love has touched my imagination
With feelings of wonder and total fascination

Looking up at so many stars that I see
Sets my mind in motion to wander free

Free to wander places near and far

Love, Sex, And Romance

As I love you through the stars

Whether we are one or thousands of miles apart
Across the stars I love you with all my heart

WOW! How they glow like my memories of you
When you look up, you will see my love shining true

And when you see them twinkling ever so bright
Your heart will know I'm thinking of you tonight

No matter where you may be, yes, wherever you are
My love will find you, on your side of the stars

STAR WRITER

ABOUT THIS POEM:

Gazing up into the stars (again!) one night, I started thinking
this crazy thought about what I would like for God to write with
the stars if I had a loved one beside me. This poem finishes
that thought.

Oh great Star Writer
What will you write tonight?
When your supreme hand touches the stars

Holding her hand, and gazing up into the night sky
Marveling at the creation of your thoughts
The splendor of your power

For as the stars light up the dark sky
So does love light up our hearts tonight
A love that burns white-hot, like the stars
It's glow seen and felt by all
Including you, The Star Writer

Wonderful Star Writer
Your magnificence is unlimited
Your mind is unsearchable
The heavens and the Earth reveal your wisdom

You have woven stars into galaxies
Blended galaxies into universes
Merged universes into eternities

And through the power of love
We are as one with these divine wonders
Under the stars tonight

Eternal Star Writer
My silent prayer to you now
With your almighty hands
May you please write
"I Love You"
With the stars tonight?

THE UNFOLDING OF THE TWO

ABOUT THIS POEM:

You know, inspiration is a funny thing. It strikes anywhere, at any time. And it can come from any source. Such was the case for this poem. It came from 2 CDs that I have from an artist named Jonn Serrie. Jonn plays some of the most beautiful music I have ever heard. Very soothing and relaxing for the soul.

The two CDs that inspired me to write this poem are titled "Midsummer Century" and "Ixlandia." (Recorded in 1993 and 1995 respectively.) These two CD's tell the story of how time and love spans eternity. On the back of the two CDs are some very beautiful poetic words that inspired me more on this poem. These two are sister CDs and I encourage you who read this poem to order them from *Miramar Music*. (Or do a *Google* search for them.)

I do not like to borrow anyone else's words and not give them credit for them. I did borrow some of the words from the poetic verses on the 2 CDs. So those will be in bold letters in the poem. I want to thank Jonn Serrie and *Miramar Music* for their lovely music and inspiring poetry.

Lastly, this poem is the first in *another* series of five about the concept of time, love, and space.

Across the mists of time
Through the limitless power of love
We have met . . .and loved

Reflections of centuries passed
And on the shores of a distant land

Our love existed

With our footprints traced in the timeline of eternity
Our souls merged into the oneness of love
The mystery of our future destiny began

As a love for the ages entwines into forever
As time and space begins the unfolding
Of the two of us

For I have loved you, as you have loved me
I unfold what I have felt of your love
Through the eons of time

The vastness of time, the deepness of love
The Two also begins their magnificent unfolding
Inside our hearts

The love of two hearts spans the greatness of time
The knowing that we have loved before in our minds

We welcome the unfolding

Ed Hendricks

THE MYSTERY OF DESTINY

ABOUT THIS POEM:

Continuing with the second poem in the second series of time, space, and love, we now see how love's destiny of the ages is fulfilled.

Across the void of infinity
Into the chasm of space and time
We existed in love
The mystery of our destiny begins

Thoughts of our love reflect into eternity
Separated beyond the expanse
The mystery of our destiny deepens

But yet, beyond this bottomless deep
I feel your presence
My heart knows you are there
I welcome your love

As eons of time passes
Universes are born and stars die out
The expanse still expands
The mystery of our destiny becomes brighter

For through all of this I have loved you
I have felt my love grow stronger
Ageless, timeless is the power of love
Now destiny unfolds its mystery

Love, Sex, And Romance

Time, the great revealer of all things
Today, this very day has shown
How much I love you
Destiny's mystery has now become reality

Ages upon ages ago I knew I loved you
You are the princess of my centuries
You are the queen of my dreams
Your love is the result of destiny's mystery revealed
My reward for an eternity of patience

And I thank you
For I have been blessed
  Forever

THE OTHER

ABOUT THIS POEM:

The third poem in this series of time, space, and love features something we all must do if we are to find our true love. What happens in space and time also happens in life and love.

As I stand at my side of the chasm
And you stand at yours
I feel you. I know you are there
And you feel me too
But yet great distances separate us

We each know we must enter this great void
If we are to meet, and love
Which will win out? Fear or the power of love?
I know what my heart feels as I step forward

But yet I wonder: Has she stepped forward too?
Has she overcome her fear of this unknown deepness?
Is the pull on her heart as strong as mine?
Does she have the courage to step forward as I have?

Moving cautiously within the void
It takes over my very being
Thrown about by its unforgiving nature
Always challenging my mind
Frustrating all my efforts to find you

In this magnificent quest of the heart

Love, Sex, And Romance

The void will test us, deny us, fail us
However persistence and determination will win out
For they will help to unite our hearts
In love

Inside space and time, we meet
I see you, know you, and love you
My heart sings joyful thanks
For your leap of faith too

For the void has done to you what it has done to me
This chasm of life's circumstances and experiences
Has changed our hearts and minds with its relentless testings
Making our love more stronger

And now, across the expanse of time
To the center of our lives today
We are now in love with

The Other

FROM THE OTHER SIDE OF TIME

ABOUT THIS POEM:

This is the fourth poem in the series of time, space, and love. I again want to thank musician Jonn Serrie for introducing this concept to me, and for his soul-inspiring music.

From the other side of time
I knew I loved you
A love so vast
A love so true

From the other side of time
I felt your love so strong
With feelings this deep
I knew they could not be wrong

From the other side of time
You opened my heart so wide
And filled it with so much
Of your tender love inside

From the other side of time
I saw your face
It made my world
A brighter and warmer place

From the other side of time
I dreamed of your touch
And when I woke from that dream

Love, Sex, And Romance

How I wanted you so much

From the other side of time
I tasted your lips
A kiss so passionate
It was worth this long trip

From the other side of time
I imagined making love to you
Beyond the highest star
You took me to

From the other side of time
I crossed the eternal expanse
For to be with you
I had to take the chance

Yesterday two hearts were separated by infinity
But I always knew one day you would be mine
And today my love has found yours across eternity
From the other side of time

Ed Hendricks

THE ETERNAL EXPANSE

ABOUT THIS POEM:

This is the last poem in the series of time, space, and love. But before I get to it, I would like to tell you about another inspiration for this type of poetry.

In the first poem in this series, I told you about a musician named Jonn Serrie who started the influence upon me to write this series of poems. Now I shall tell you of another musician who influenced me, to end this series of poetry.

Steve Roach is this musician's name and he creates lush, deep atmospheres with sound (or Space music, as its genre is titled.) I often listen to his work as I am working late into the night. One of my favorites by him is titled "The Eternal Expanse" in which he and four other artists create this world of sound that takes you to the deepest parts of outer space and your inner mind.

I like to listen to this type of music for it frees my mind to go beyond the Earth and to the deepest parts of space and into myself as well. So if this poetry seems "deep," this is the reason why.

I want to thank you as well, Steve Roach, for your inspiring and soul-stirring music.

My love,
When I gaze up into a star-filled night

And wonder...
How vast is eternity
How endless is infinity

How deep is my love for you
For space itself grows larger by the day
And the cosmos is forever expanding
The vastness of the expanse inspires my imagination
To love you more every day

The passing of countless eons of time
The birth and death of billions of stars
The creation of unlimited galaxies
The forming of ageless universes
The splendid blessing of being in love with you
All of these wonders exist within

The eternal expanse

Special note: The Time and Love concept poems in this
section will be will be the centerpiece for my second book titled
"Knights of Brave Love: The Courageous Quest for Her
Eternal Heart."

INTERLUDE: A NIGHT SO SPECIAL

What is it about the night that inspires and intensifies romance? In the realm of love, it is the night that has inspired great poets, writers, and storytellers the most. Who has not read a romantic story in which a star-filled night was a part of it? How about a candlelit dinner followed by a specially prepared room, lit up by candles? Even in the movies and on television, a night filled with love and passion is featured often. And many love songs are about love and the night.

One of my favorite 80s movies is "Urban Cowboy," which starred John Travolta and Debra Winger. There was a night scene in it in which John Travolta and his new lover were up in her apartment having a drink by a window, overlooking the city. You could see the city lights at night in the background as the two of them shared a kiss together.

While all this was happening, the song "Love, Look What You Done to Me" by Boz Scaggs was playing. This scene (to me) was one of the most romantic night love scenes I've ever seen in a movie.

The point I'm trying to make here is that for those who are in love, the night can be the most rewarding time they can spend together. And after a long day working along with its cares and worries, the night can be such a special time for lovers to open their minds and hearts to each other.

Never forget the magic that the night can hold. The possibilities are endless.

CANDLELIGHT, MOONLIGHT, STARLIGHT

ABOUT THIS POEM:

The title of this poem speaks for its subject. It is about those romantic lights of the night. I wanted to take each of those splendid lights and make them into their own mini poem and at the same time make them all a part of one larger romantic poem.

CANDLELIGHT

On a night so warm as a gentle breeze blows
Candles light up the room with their mystical glow

Candles in the room gave off their magical light
Entices you and me with their splendid sight

Feelings of love take over our control
Loving each other mind, body, and soul

In love so deep and it feels so right
We celebrate our love on this very special night

The candles are lit up like stars in the room
We turn on mellow music, to play a romantic tune

The stage is set for a night of love
When the moon comes out from above

MOONLIGHT

The moon starts its journey across the night sky
We step outside into the darkness

Its presence adds to the romance
Of this beautiful night

Slowly moving majestically across the night sky
We drink in its spherical splendor
Its glow lights up the darkness
Like our love does

United in love under this natural wonder
Two hearts encircled in the fullness of love
But the moon also has a celestial audience
Created by the magnificent Star Writer

STARLIGHT

As the moon lights the way
And the stars come out to play
In awe we have to say

"My God, what a grand sight
For the moon and the stars are out tonight"
They add to our love feeling so right

How bright the stars shine
Heavenly wonders so fine
Tonight, how glad I am that you are mine

Look! There and there and everywhere
The stars come out from their hidden lair
The night sky is no longer bare

Holding your lovely hand
Outside tonight we stand
Gazing up into a magnificent wonderland

Thank you God for setting them free
The many stars we can see
We revel in tonight's destiny

On this marvelous night
When space, time, and nature unfolds
And combines with love
So blessed are we in this revealing celebration
Of our love tonight

Candlelight, Moonlight, Starlight
All magnify the glory of their creator
So too, does our love

THIEVES OF TIME (STOLEN MOMENTS)

ABOUT THIS POEM:

I wrote this poem about a couple who are in love and want to spend some time alone together but their everyday lives are so busy. So one night they just steal away by themselves to rekindle their love. With the frantic and hectic world we live in, it is so easy for us to become so caught up in the rush that we neglect our love. So this poem goes out to all those lovers whose lives are so busy that they yearn for one special night together. A night together that they will always remember and cherish.

Also, after listening to the song "Steal Away" by Robbie Dupree, I then realized that this poem goes perfect with that song. I have always loved this song since I heard it in the 80s and to be able to write a poem that goes with it is truly a blessing.

The moments we spend together for us two
Are priceless and precious, but so few

For being with you is of the utmost matter
But like leaves in the wind our time is scattered

So busy are our nights and days
To everything and everyone else does time we pay

With our lives so full of its daily grind
So lost is the time together we find

Love, Sex, And Romance

And as we drift further and further apart
My greatest fear is that I'm losing your heart

It would be so kind
If we could just find
Some moments in time
For our hearts to again bind
And it will serve to remind
That we still have each other's love in mind

And after one long, hard day
I come to you and say
"Honey, let's just steal away"
To our own private place of play
For the rest of today"
Once there, we will lovingly stay

And as dusk approaches, so goes the light
We steal away, like thieves in the night

It doesn't matter where we go
Long as I'm with you it's joy I will know

We'll forget our "other life" with its worries and cares
And spend this time together to lay our souls bare

With our hearts in each other's hands
We now enter into our secret wonderland

For now we have stolen away
To a place where "they" can't touch us
Where two hearts beat as one
Where by space and time we are no longer bound

Ed Hendricks

Where our very souls combine and entwine
Where our spirits flow and let go
Until we are now...

As one

Now we have stolen away like thieves in the night
Gracefully, easily like two birds in flight

Just like Ali Baba and the 40 thieves
We too, have stolen as we please

For these moments are ours and ours alone
To hold each other close
To share our dreams
Our cares
Our fears
Our tears
Our rights
Our wrongs
Our prayers
Our songs
To share our love
To make love
To stare and wonder at the stars above
To joke
To laugh
To act like the children we were in the past
To plan
To heal
To once again our love seal

Father Time, to us, nothing you have lent

Love, Sex, And Romance

You we had to steal, and away we went

Why did you have to treat us so unkind?
For it was moments like these you did undermine

You took from us one of life's greatest pleasures
The time alone we value and treasure

But we have taken something back from you
For the memories of this night will see us through

This is one night I wish would never end
Spending this time with my lover, my best friend

But deep in the night as the shadows have fallen
We begin to hear slumber's unwelcome calling

And as we sleep through this mythical night
Content in our hearts, as it felt so right

When morning shines its glorious face
We'll wake and remember going away to our secret place

To the next day and the next and the next
These moments will be the bright spot in our lives so complex

Through these days we will take time to reflect
On the night when time we did circumspect

And to you my love, these memories I'll bind
The moments we stole away, like thieves of time.

Ed Hendricks

WHISPERS AND SURRENDERS

ABOUT THIS POEM:

On a night filled with passion, words are said as emotions are overloaded. This poem is my expression in words about those tender moments.

Embraced within the night
We are wrapped around each other
Giggling, laughing, talking
Stolen kisses. One, then another
And another
And another
Suddenly they are longer
And longer
And longer
We get lost in their intensity
And their passion

A breathless "I love you so much" escape from your lips
A whisper so sweet
I return it with a kiss

As the flames of desire take over
And they grow more intense, more forceful
More whispers, more kisses
More promises of eternal love

Whisper to me your greatest thoughts
Your sensual secrets

Love, Sex, And Romance

And I will do the same

Surrender to me that special place in your heart

Again, I will do the same

Now the surrender begins

Another heartfelt "I love you" in the dark
Cuts through the lust and into my heart

Moments of passion between us two
Makes the bond of love stronger between me and you

Giving into the heat of love we have made
An ecstasy so wonderful that is no longer delayed

A surrender so sweet, and so fine
Merging together our bodies, souls, and minds

And when we awaken to the light of the next day
I will gaze into your lovely eyes and say

"Honey, I will always remember
Last night's beautiful whispers and surrenders"

OF LOVE AND DREAMS

ABOUT THIS POEM:

The inspiration for this poem came from several places. The very first line of this poem came to me while I was thinking about the poem "Inside Her Eyes" which was featured earlier in this book. Then a few more lines of this poem just popped into my head and I took it from there.

Also to add to this, I wrote a poem in 1993 titled "As She Lays Sleep" which deals with this same subject. That poem was only the second poem I ever wrote. I rewrote it years later and changed it into this one.

And lastly, I want to dedicate this poem to my friend Talma Xavier of Recife, Brazil. For without her inspiration, this poem would still be a rough draft. I sent her the first three verses of this poem and she loved them. So I told her I would "give" this poem to her. Obrigado Muitas (many thanks) Talma!

A dream so deep, is where you now abide
As you lay softly sleeping by my side

In a land filled with enchantment, is where you now exist
For you heard the call of sleep, and could not resist

I gaze fondly at you, as you sleep
And ask myself "What dreams do you keep?"

For I long to be with you in that magical land

Love, Sex, And Romance

As together we face your dreams, hand in hand

To fly with you places great and far
To glide with you through the stars

To help calm you from what you fear
To share with you what you hold dear

To plan with you, your highest goal
To be the thief with you, as time we stole

To keep you safe and out of harm's way
To laugh and act like children, as we play

When the morning light comes and you wake from your dream
Back from a place where things are not as they seem

You turn to me with eyes so misty
And say "Thank you Honey for being there with me"

THE QUEEN OF MY DREAMS

ABOUT THIS POEM:

The poem I wrote titled "The Mystery of Destiny" (Page 76) has a verse in it that reads:

"Ages upon ages ago I knew I loved you
For you are the princess of my centuries
You are the queen of my dreams"

So I took that last line and made it into its own love poem.

In the kingdom of my dreams
Where my life plays on my mind's screen
You are my queen

Thinking of you throughout the day
And as the light fades away
Now my imagination has full play

In this realm of the night
My heart takes to flight
How this feels, ever so right

Like the tales of knights of old
Brave at heart with courage so bold
My love for you is a story that must be told

But loving you is not a fairy tale
It is a feeling that I know so well

And deep in my heart is where it dwells

My nights are filled with thoughts of you
As well as the day we just loved through
And I know you feel this too

You are my queen, I am your knight
Like a hero, for your love I will fight
Even when my mind turns off its light

And at the end of your nightly reign
When I return to daylight's plane
The love for my queen will forever remain

Special note: The bold print parts of this poem will be very much featured in my second book titled: Knights of Brave Love: The Courageous Quest for Her Eternal Heart. Stay tuned!

INTERLUDE: LOVE AND SEX

This is a topic that can be debated and discussed almost endlessly. And in the end, will any definite solution be reached? So for our purpose here in this book, we will stay on the positive side of this subject.

It is natural that when two people are in love, sooner or later sex will enter the picture. When in love, giving yourself to your partner sexually is the ultimate expression of your love for that person. It is the merging of two bodies, two minds, and two souls into one ecstatic union.

Sex in love is supposed to make a relationship deeper, stronger and yes, more enjoyable. But sex alone is not enough to keep a relationship strong. Sex only deepens love. Good love. I know of couples that have said the only good thing they had in common in their relationship was sex. Needless to say other areas of their lives together were a mess.

Those couples just prove that sex alone will not make a good relationship. But sex can make a good relationship better, and a better one deeper. This can only happen with the greatest force for good known to humanity.

The power of love.

MAKING LOVE TO HER

ABOUT THIS POEM:

This is a poem I wrote to tell the men of the world that there are other ways than the act of sex to make love to a woman. What I am also trying to say here is that sex starts in the mind. I do believe that you have to make love to the mind FIRST, and then the body will follow willingly.

Also, the idea of all day foreplay I write about in this poem is not new. Number 391 in the book "1001 Ways to be Romantic" by Gregory Godek (and Casablanca Press) goes along with my thinking here. I *strongly* recommend this book (and of course, my book too!) for all romantic, deep hearted thinkers and lovers.

Morning . . . a new day begins
I turn over and look lovingly at her
As she lays sleep

The thought comes up
Why not breakfast in bed?
Is she not worth it?

Toast, bacon, eggs, hot coffee
gives you a splendid surprise
When you awaken

That look in your eyes
A deep, soulful kiss

Ed Hendricks

Sends us off to work

I pass by a flower shop
So red are the roses
They remind me of your heart

Early afternoon, a call from you
Excited and delighted is your voice
The roses are beautiful

A little love note hidden in your purse
lightly scented with my cologne
You read and inhale with a smile

Off from work early
I am home doing housework
Your dinner is almost ready

You and the roses breeze through the door
Our eyes and lips meet
I eagerly look forward to tonight

Dinner, the roses, the candles
The talk is lively
You like my cooking

"No, no, Honey
I will do the dishes"
You save your strength . . . for later

Come, our bubble bath is ready
The water feels great
Just like you

Love, Sex, And Romance

Drying each other off
The towel lingers at certain spots
Our senses come alive

Lit candles in the bedroom
We draw each other close
A night of romance has begun

As other emotions subside and love arise
As two bodies become one and inhibitions are undone
As passion implodes and ecstasy explodes

I realize . . .

I have been making love to her all day long

INSTANT SEX, ALWAYS LOVE

ABOUT THIS POEM:

I have always wanted to write an erotic, sexual poem. This poem is the result of that thinking. A reader asked me if this poem really happened. My answer was . . .

On a special sunny afternoon
I see you standing by the window
Alluring, enticing, exciting
Your eyes meet mine with the look of longing
Come closer, closer still they tell me
Touch me, caress me
Take me

Soft kisses start the tingle
Anticipation of love and more
A hint of your perfume
Raises my excitement

Breaths get short
Kisses get long
Hands that stroked faces
Now find secret places
Body temperatures rise
Clothes now fall
Sweat on skin meets sweat on skin

You lead me to the sofa and then you lay down
Exposing your luscious, blooming glory to me

Love, Sex, And Romance

I drink of your nectar so sweet
For thirsty I am of your love

Cries of unrestrained passion come from your lips
Spasms of a star-filled rapture overcomes you
Again and again

But your hunger is not satisfied
Neither is mine
Pulled down on top of you
A sense of urgent need your touch has
In more places than one

Easily, I fill you with myself
Gasps of delightful pleasure escape our control
You draw more of me into you
Into your magnificent world of seduction
A gentle flowing rhythm of two bodies begins
Two hearts, two minds, two souls
Merge into one, move as one
In harmony with space and time

What started as an easy rhythm
Now becomes a relentless drive
Your moans fill my senses
Your body wrapped around mine
I am the hammer of lust
Striking the nail of your sex
But you as the nail also strikes back
Pounding each other into a quivering ecstasy

As the dam bursts and flows into the river
And the river overflows its shores once more

Ed Hendricks

Our blissful journey to the stars ends, leaving us in a romantic afterglow

Two hearts will always know and feel
How much they are in love

BEAUTIFUL MUSIC, BEAUTIFUL LOVE (THE AFTERGLOW)

ABOUT THIS POEM:

After making love one afternoon and catching my breath, the title to this poem came to me. (Remember earlier I said that inspiration can come at any time, any place!) So I wanted to write about my feelings on an afternoon I will never forget, and will always treasure.

In the light of a slow, sunny afternoon

Soft music plays, we are off work today
Romance calls, clothes fall
Lips meet, hearts skip beats
Bodies touch, pulses rush
Making love starts and we both do our parts
Passion unfolds, ecstasy explodes
Climaxes are peaked and it's rest we now seek

Holding you close after the love we made
Enjoying the feeling of the passion we obeyed

Basking in the glow of something so beautiful
This for us was much more than physical

Mental, emotional, spiritual it was all of these combined
The ultimate expression of our love this moment in time

Energy is drained as we lay gasping for air

Ed Hendricks

I now stroke your lovely hair

Beautiful music plays in the background
Helps to calm the body rush down

Snuggled around each other, feeling our hearts beat
The afterglow makes this love complete

And as that warmth covers us like a slow moving fire
Puts the finishing touch to our desires

The music, the love, and an afterglow so fine
We eagerly look forward to the next time

Love, Sex, And Romance

THE BODY REMEMBERS

ABOUT THIS POEM:

I like most forms of music, but jazz is one of my favorites. Some time ago I heard a jazz song by Lorraine Feather, which was the same title of this poem. Years later, when writing this poem, I thought of that song and thought that the song title would also make a good poem title.

As I sit here and think about you...

My eyes remember when I looked at you
They light up like two stars in the night do

My breath gets short as I gaze in awe
At the beautiful and lovely woman that you are

My hands want to reach out to caress your cheek
My ears can't wait to hear you speak

How I yearn to run my fingers through your hair
Gently, tenderly, and with loving care

My arms want to be around you entwined
Our two bodies become as one combined

My lips long to be touching yours
When they meet, my pulse starts to soar

Now love turns into ecstasy

Ed Hendricks

I realize I am living my fantasy

Desire takes over as we move together
God, how I wish this could last forever

Now we take each other to wonderful heights of pleasure
My mind remembers why it's you I treasure

As passion explodes into flames of a white hot hue
My heart remembers how much I love you

DAYS OF LONGING, NIGHTS OF PASSION

ABOUT THIS POEM:

There are times when you are in love with someone so much and so deep, that you cannot stop thinking about them, day or night. I try to tell about some of those feelings here in this poem.

Another day begins anew
The sun awakens from its temporary slumber
So too does my love for you

Like the day, the yearning again starts
My body and mind ache with want
Soul and spirit do their part

Spending time with you intensifies the thirst
Pleasing laughter, gentle touches, respectful talk
Always knowing my love for you comes first

All day I craved your love so much
Your smile, your laugh, your charming personality
How I hungered to feel that rush

Now the night is finally here
My mind anticipates total joy
Wanting so much to hold you near

This wonderful feeling of sweet delight
When I gaze into your eyes of forever

As the passion between us begins to ignite

Desire turns into pure lust
Two bodies become one
Giving into our needs we now must

My day of longing is no longer fantasy
The stars now come into view
We reach the highest point of ecstasy

May the days of longing for you more and more
Make me look forward to
Nights with so much passion in store

APPLE PIE LOVE

ABOUT THIS POEM:

This is one of those goofy little poems that may leave a smile on your face. While cooking dinner in the kitchen one day, an ex and I got a little frisky, and...well... just read on and find out.

Making chili with you late one afternoon
The radio plays smooth jazz tunes

Laughing, joking, teasing, just having fun
Knowing in my heart that you are the one

The one I want to love, forevermore
The one I want to forever adore

"Honey, please put the pie in the oven
Then come over here and give me some lovin' "

To the refrigerator, rushes I
And take out an apple pie

Out of the box and into the stove so fast
And turn it on to start the heat blast

I then turn to you and see that look in your eye
No words need to be spoken for we both know why

In the middle of the kitchen we start to kiss

Ed Hendricks

Suddenly the phone rings..." WHO IS THIS??? "

A friend with a problem crashes the mood
Thirty minutes later, the house smells of food

And as the smell of the pie fills the house
I playfully try to take off your blouse

You whisper "Wait til' I get off the phone"
So sexy you are, I just can't leave you alone

Finally you finish the interrupting call
And we waste no more time, as clothes now fall

We follow the clothes down to the floor
The fire of desire now turns to a roar

The aroma of the pie hot and baking
Also adds something new to the love we are making

Soon, our ecstasies reach their highest peak
We lay gasping on the floor, for rest to seek

Catching our breath on the floor of the kitchen
This was fantastic . . . magical . . . truly bewitching

Then the timer on the stove starts to buzz
Bringing us out of our apple pie love

INTERLUDE: A MAN IN LOVE

We men have a lot to learn about love and loving. We have to learn to open up our hearts more and let our finer emotions shine through. Some in society feel when a man expresses his loving emotions, he is "weak" or a "sissy" or "whipped" or even a "punk."

Friends may even tease him or give him one of those names mentioned earlier. Thus he may feel as if he should not open his heart up to his loved one. When this happens, "manly pride" sets in and there will be troubles ahead.

I want to tell the men of the world that there is NOTHING wrong with showing how much you are in love. And if you must take teasing and ridicule, SO BE IT! IS SHE NOT WORTH IT?

I want the world to know that yes, I am in love with this woman, and yes, I will open my heart up to her and yes, if you do not like it, then TOUGH! DEAL WITH IT!

At the same time in defense of men, I have to say that there is a danger of being taken advantage of by your loved one. She just might think that you do fit one of those labels and use that against you. There is a time to be a gentleman and a time to be a man.

It is not easy for most men to open their hearts to the one they love. So when we do, it is deeply personal and it exposes our vulnerability and fears.

And one more point I would like to touch on, is that many women think that men think with too much intellect and logic.

And there is also the thought that we men only think with one particular lower body part! Yes, that may be true with *some* men, but not with *all* men.

Give us some credit ladies. We may not think like a woman but we do have the same emotions as a woman. We just use them differently. We too can love just as much, and maybe even more deeply as you can. (I believe this book proves the point!)

Men of the world, be brave. Open your hearts up and love. Win or lose, succeed or fail. Don't they say that it is better to have lost at love than not to have loved at all?

JUST A MAN

ABOUT THIS POEM:

This is a poem I wrote about us men and our insecurities. At times we feel as if we are not good enough to be in love with a woman. Doubts come up because we place her on a pedestal so high that it makes us feel inferior to her. In this poem, I will try to explain those feelings.

I AM...

Just a man
Who wants to love you
Body and soul
Heart and mind
To love you with all I have
Spiritually, mentally, physically
To be in love with you
Day and night, always falling

For I am...

Just a man
A man whom is searching for the face of God
By doing what is right
By treating you right
That He may bless our love
So that we have a chance
To be together forever
Living and loving

For I am....

Just a man
A man who fights his fears
That he is not good enough

To love someone like you
Totally, completely, unconditionally
A man who yearns to touch your delicate skin
To hold your lovely body
To kiss your fair lips
To make love with you so passionately
For he feels so unworthy
Of such a marvelous beauty
Of such a natural splendor

For I am...

Just a man
Who longs to be closer than close to you
So near, but yet so far away
When I am with you
Into your mind is where I long to be
My hiding place is within your heart

Can this man be given the chance to do all these things with you?
For you? To you?
Can you forgive this man's shortcomings?
His fears?
His tears?

Will you hold him when he cries over you?

Will you scold him when you're mad at him?
But most importantly, will you still love him?
For I am...

Just a man

Ed Hendricks

THE HANDS OF A MAN

ABOUT THIS POEM:

This is a poem I wrote for all the men out there in the world
that does manual work with their hands. I am talking about the
auto mechanics, construction workers, carpenters, janitors,
farmers, plumbers, gardeners, etc., etc. Those of us who do
hard with our hands have the scars and the ailments to prove
it. Yet our hands still have a "soft" side that we want our loved
one to know about. This is my attempt to tell about that soft
side.

Gazing at my hands
The years of toil tells on them
Working on this, working on that
They have paid the price

Hands that have done both good and bad
Hands that have done things they shouldn't have

Hands that have played and hands that have prayed
Hands that have fought hard and now are frayed

But now a blessing has come into these hands
A splendid treasure that is oh, so grand

For the love of a woman has been placed in them
In these hands a love like this has never been

A lovely thing of beauty and such grace

118

Love, Sex, And Romance

In this man's hands your love feels out of place

For how could these hands wrought with life's steel
Have opened your heart and to again love feel

How could such hands give you a loving touch
Together with its mind is in love with you so much

How could hands like this make love to you
When it's hard work that they are used to

But the hands of this man are asking for a chance
To light up your eyes and make your heart dance

The hands of this man are begging for a chance
To love you so much that your mind is entranced

The hands of this man pleads for the chance
To give you respect, honor, and yes even romance

But most importantly...

Will this man have the chance in his life
To hold your hand in his, as man and wife?

Ed Hendricks

THE MAN THAT YOU DESERVE

ABOUT THIS POEM:

This is a poem that I wrote to a friend of mine named Teri, who was going through a rough time with a boyfriend of hers. He was really mistreating her and causing her much grief. She called me up one night after one of his rants. At one point in our talk, I told her that she deserves better than him and it's about time she found it without him. But I have to ask: Do not we all deserve the best of love? Should we settle for being treated any less? At this time I wish to send this poem out to ALL who know they deserve the best of love, like my friend Teri.

Also, this was one of the most difficult poems I ever wrote. What I tried to do was to use four lines per verse, and each line had to rhyme at the end. To do this and keep the subject of the poem straight was a challenge for me.

He is a fortunate man
Who has your world in the palm of his hands
If he can but understand
That it's going to take everything he can

To be that special one
To give his all and then some
To make sure to you total right is done
To make your heart shine in the sun

From the deepest, darkest part of the night

Love, Sex, And Romance

To the highest point of daylight
When your day shines so bright
He must try with all his might

To show you how much he cares
And he will always be there
Whether the going is good or fair
To find such a man is truly rare

For the road your heart has taken has been rocky and long
And has had more than its fair share of wrongs
Now your heart sings the sad song
Of how the two of you did not get along

Little by little from the start
Then piece-by-piece he broke your heart
Slowly but surely you drifted apart
From your life now he must depart

For you to now be free
From that which was not meant to be
For now you clearly can see
That the man you deserve was not he

To my words please do heed
The man that you need
Will come forth with dashing speed
With truth and respect in word, thought, and deed
So that your heart may never again bleed

To forget his own and help you with your pain
That in your heart may still remain
Any further hurt to you he will refrain

Ed Hendricks

For he does not want your face tear stained

He must reach into his own heart's reserve
For it's your love he is trying to preserve
And when you find this man to your heart he will serve
Is truly the man that you deserve

LOVE LETTER #9

ABOUT THIS LETTER:

When going to school, I remember those third grade love letters I wrote to a girl named Shari and how childish they were. So here I am years later, writing another love letter in the "school of life" in which we all are students of. But as you will see, my love letters have grown up quite a bit.

Music also helped me to title this letter. There are songs titled "Love Potion #9" by The Clovers (and later by The Searchers) and "Situation #9" by Club Nouveau. So I thought "Why not Love Letter #9?"

My darling,

I am writing you another letter to tell you I love you and to tell you how much I am in love with you.

Everything about you I have fallen in love with and I look forward to falling deeper in love with you. Your sexy walk, the charming way you talk, your delicious scent, your melodic laugh, and those dreamy eyes! When I gaze into them, I feel my heart and infinity combine as one, as I try to search through your eyes to find the center of your ever-loving heart.

When I am with you I feel like I am a child again. So playful, carefree and easy.

Making love with you reminds me of two eternal flowing rivers coming together with no effort to form one beautiful body in motion. You always know how to take me to a realm of bliss and ecstasy that exists above the stars.

No other person has ever made me feel this way. You have awakened my senses, inspired my dreams, and excited my fantasies. How blessed I am to have fallen in love with you so much and to know that you feel the same.

When I look up at the stars in the night, I imagine I see two stars sparkling much brighter than the rest, shining side-by-side. Suddenly they start moving closer and closer to each other until they become one majestic, bright glowing ball of light. I feel that you and I were those two stars shining on our own. But now that we are together, we have become that one great glowing star whose light the world can see.

Can you see how much I love you? Can you feel the words of this letter from my heart to yours? This is what you loving me the way you do has done to me.

Honey, I could go on writing this letter for days or even for weeks telling you so much more about how much I love you. So I will close with these words.

If ever you doubt that I love you or how much I am in love with you, then please read this letter again. And know that I love you even more now since the first time you read this letter.

With all my love,

Ed

OH TEACHER

ABOUT THIS POEM:

When two people first fall in love, there is that time period in which they are getting to know each other's likes and dislikes. I feel that you should teach each other about those likes and dislikes. To teach each other how to love each other. For my part, I want to be taught by her. How to love her in the way she wants to be loved. And this poem tells about me wanting to learn.

When I was young and going through school
Being taught the Golden Rule

English, science, reading, math
Were the subjects of my path

But in school I never did learn
How to love a woman and her heart to earn

Now out of school and living my life
And loving the woman who will be my wife

When the pupil is ready, the teacher will appear
My best friend, my lover, you are now here

So my dear, please teach me too
What is the best way to love you

To adore you in the way you deserve

For our love to always preserve

Teach me how to play my part
In the keeping of your heart

Please lead my mind in the right direction
So I may shower you with joy with and affection

Teach me how you yearn to make love
So our passion will explode into the stars above

Bring out in me all my best
To give you all my love and nothing less

Discipline me with your loving might
So I will know how to love you right

Oh teacher, a willing student I will be
Dedicated to you eternally

So please enroll me in your life's class
And teach me well, so I will forever pass

TO BE

ABOUT THIS POEM:

Some years ago, I read the following lines of poetry on a poetry site online: "If I were to die tonight I would want to come back as one of your tears. Who would not want to be conceived in your heart, born in your eye, live on your cheek and die on your lips?"

Such beautiful words inspired my mind to make a whole poem out of them. I changed some of those words from those lines so that they would fit into this poem better, but I made sure I kept the original meaning. I also looked on the internet to find out who *first* wrote these words so I could give them proper credit, but could not find that person. So if any of you dear readers know who *first* wrote those lines and what poem (if any) they came from, please let me know so I can gladly give them the credit they deserve.

To be a joyful tear, born in your eye
To live on your cheek
To die on your lips
Oh so sweet of a death

To be a rose, softly touched by you
Its fragrant scent, deeply inhaled by you
Its petals compared to your heart

To be the sun, that shines down upon you
To be that ray, that touches your skin

To be thought of, as its warmth spreads over you

To be the star, that shines in your nights
Its glow lights up your imagination
As you gaze up and wonder…

To be the thought inside your mind
That lights up your beautiful face
Into a glowing smile

To be the passion in your life
That inspires and excites you
To help you achieve your goals

To be the man, that you deserve*
Loving and respecting you, like a true man should
And receiving the same

To be the best I can be
To love you, and so much more
For in your life, I am asking for more than just…

　To be

* A reference to the poem "The Man That You Deserve" on page 120.

831

ABOUT THIS POEM:

This poem is about the words "I LOVE YOU".
8 Letters
3 Words
1 Meaning

Also, when you text message someone "831," you are telling them "I love you."

I LOVE YOU

8 letters that say so much
And mean even more
The glory of any alphabet
Is revealed with these letters
By themselves, these letters mean nothing
But when they are put together
They tell what I know and feel
Inside my heart, mind, and spirit

   For....

I LOVE YOU

3 words that 8 letters have formed
Words that when I say to you
Come from my soul, my very being
As wide as the sky, as deep as the ocean

As tall as the mountains, as vast as the stars
As high as the heavens
The only way I can give you those wonders is through these 3 words

For....

I LOVE YOU

1 Meaning

Totally
Deeply
Unconditionally
All questions have been answered

Enough said

I CAN ONLY LOVE YOU LIKE THIS

ABOUT THIS POEM:

I wrote this poem about and to those men who are told that they love too deeply and that they should just "love on the surface." I want to tell them here in this poem (and in this section *and* in this book) that there is nothing wrong with loving deeply with everything you have inside.

Completely, faithfully
Playfully, joyfully
Unconditionally
Is the only ways I can love you

With every beat of my heart
Every part of my soul
Every ounce of my spirit
All of me I give all to you
For this is the best way I know how to love you

A simple man I am
Who yearns to love you so tender
Who pleads to fall in love with you so deep
Who dreams to make love with you so passionate
To love you with everything
Takes true courage and great confidence
For the hero of your heart I stand to be

Small minds will say I love you too much
I give you too much and then some

In the name of love

Is this not what true love is?
Don't you deserve to be loved like this?
To be wanted? Desired?

I do not care what they think or say
I will stand firm in the face of criticism
Then rise above it

I want to always love you and adore you so much
This is the only way I can love you
Always more, never less
All I ask from you
Is the same

LOVE SPELL

ABOUT THIS POEM:

Victoria's Secret has a perfume named "Love Spell." I smelled it one time and it smelled so good and exciting. Inspiration then took over as I thought that the title would make a good love poem.

When I sit and think about you
And all the magical things you do

I search the depths of my mind
To find out why I think of you all the time

I think I know what the answer could be
To this heartfelt mystery

I do know how I fell
Under the wonders of your love spell

When I met you right from the start
Honey, I knew you had my heart

With a pair of bewitching eyes
You took my heart by surprise

Lips that resemble red nectar so sweet
Desire told me mine had to meet

And when I heard your spellbinding voice

My heart leaped high with rejoice

When you entranced me with your personality
It was then you totally had me

Now my resistance has been made frail
By the power of your love spell

A sorceress of the heart you are
For you have enchanted my thoughts, by far

Like a magician with a bag of tricks
You pulled out your love, and made it stick

Captured I am by your love so mystical
What I feel for you is much deeper than physical

Such a strong spell over me you cast
My wish is forever that it will last

PLAY IN LOVE

ABOUT THIS POEM:

This poem is about those not-so-serious moments in love. Those light-hearted times which we all need when in love. Our everyday lives tend to make us all tense and stressed out, so we may take out those negative emotions on the one we adore. Therefore, we all must learn to lighten up and "play in love."

Oh lover,
That joke was so funny
Thanks so much for sharing it with me

I love to see your face light up
I love to hear you laugh
This tells me that we can still have fun together

Let us not let the responsibilities of adulthood take away our childlike nature
For the kids we once were we can become again

I love to have fun with you
Whatever that may be
Watching our favorite comedy on TV
Going out to a movie

Let's play a game of pool together
Bowling anyone?
How about miniature golf, my love?

"Awww, you missed a three foot putt"
I say in mock sorrow/smile

Let's go to an amusement park and scream like kids as we ride
A game of cards? A board game? A puzzle?
Crazy dancing to our favorite song
Tickling, teasing, touching

Let's see the world together
Let's share this play world together
Let's delight in those lighthearted moments
For they will draw us even closer

In love

TALK TO ME

ABOUT THIS POEM:

I will come right out and say that the inspiration of this poem came from the failure of my first marriage. We did not have any good communication and it helped to end our marriage. (There is another BIG reason why it ended too, which we will not discuss). As I look back on the mistakes that were made, **the lack of good talking to each other was *the* key**. So I wanted to use this poem as a lesson for ALL of us, telling all to talk to the one you love with respect and with love.

My love, can we please talk?
For I want to know what's on your mind
What's in your heart
And the depths of your soul

Your highest dreams
Your secret fantasies
Your deepest fears
Your biggest laughs
I would like to know these
And in return, I will tell you the same

Also, it's not what we say, but how we say it
So may we always have . . .

Open talk
Honest talk
Respectful talk

Two-way talk

Honey, I love you so much
And I am in love with you so much
Is it wrong to want to know your feelings about life and about
us?

For what happens to you happens to me
When you hurt and are in pain
So am I
When you are happy and laughing
So am I
Entwined we are in life and in love
Together forever can be our destiny
Closer than close we draw to each other
When we talk

WHAT DID HE DO?

ABOUT THIS POEM:

When you see a couple together you sometimes wonder not only how they came together but also what were the feelings and emotions that attracted them to each other. These are questions I sometimes ask myself when I see two people in love. But I really pose this question to the woman. And in this poem, I try to answer it.

Also, this questioning poem goes out to those who thought they had the love of another person, only to lose it to someone else.

Watching the two of you together
Wondering if it will last forever

I ask myself "What did he do?"
To win the heart of someone like you

Was it something about his face?
That made your pulse start to race

Was it something in his eyes?
That gave your heart a delightful surprise

Could it have been in his voice?
That now makes your heart rejoice

Was it the way he held your hand?

Ed Hendricks

That made you see he was the man

Or was it something in his kiss?
That made you realize what you miss

Let me guess, just maybe
It was his personality?

Clothes, money, cars, those shallow material things
Are they the reason you now wear his ring?

Such a lucky man is he
To have won your love totally

From afar, I give him my best
For he passed all your tests

Like an actor playing his best part
He won the award for your heart

Yes, of all of these questions I ask of you
The one still remains: "What did he do?"

FROM AFAR

ABOUT THIS POEM:

This poem goes out to those of us who love someone from a distance, but yet are too scared to go up and say anything. As you will see in the poem, one of the reasons for this fear is what others may think and say. Another reason is rejection. So we keep the feelings to ourselves.

As I watch you every day pass by
Your walk, your talk, your smile, your laugh
My heart saddens as you leave for the day
The longing already starts to see you again tomorrow

From afar, I love you
A secret buried deep within
For outside, ridicule would be the words
Said by those who don't understand

For I feel I have loved you through the ages
My Timeless Princess
As then and as now
My love has not failed

When I leave, I take you with me
Through my imagination we live
A nighttime of dreams awaits me
Being in love with you

Maybe one day true courage will arise

And I reveal to you these feelings
But again tomorrow, as like every day

I will love you

From afar

SPECIAL FEATURE: WORLD LOVE POEMS

I want to first say that the inspiration for this section comes from my favorite NPR radio program "The World." (Special thanks to PRI, The BBC, and WGBH Boston. They all also help to sponsor and put on this insightful radio show.) I am a loyal and faithful listener and I have learned so much about the world and the people in it. I especially love the "Geo Quiz" for I sometimes get some of the answers right!

While listening to it one night, the thought came to me to write some poems about (and to) the women of the world. So that is what I did here in this section.

I took some of the countries and regions of the world and wrote these special poems about the women who live in them. I wish I could have written about the women in all the countries of the world, but unfortunately I could not. So if your country or region is not in these poems, please do not feel left out. Know that you have my respect and admiration too.

And once again, music backs up my thinking on this particular subject. Two songs that were very popular come to mind. They are: "Mrs. Right" by Mindless Behavior and "International Love" by Pitbull, featuring Chris Brown.

LADY OF AFRICA

ABOUT THIS POEM:

I would like to start our journey around the world with Africa. And to tell the women in Africa that you are held in high esteem no matter what has happened or is happening in some of your countries.

In a region full of sun
You add to its glow
And its warmth

Grand is your spirit, dear lady
You deserve the respect of the world
For your struggles
Your bravery
Your determination
Are what legends are made of

The world can look up to you as an example
Of these fine qualities
Heroes you have become
For your integrity has awakened the compassion of many

Faithful lady
I will plea to God with you, and for you
To keep your soul close to his own
For inside his eyes
You are still his queen
Yesterday, today, and forevermore

LADY OF AMERICA

ABOUT THIS POEM:

This poem is for the women of America, to let them all know how much admiration I have for them.

Also, there is a story behind the two lines in bold print in this poem. While listening to "The World" one evening, a story came on about some young girls in a far-off village in India, who were taking boxing lessons and looked up to, and were inspired by the former American Women's Boxing Champion Laila Ali. I then thought to myself, "How cool is this, that these girls so far away in India are inspired by this great American lady?

Dearest American lady
From a land that spans between two oceans
And all the natural wonders within
Does not your heart compare to these?

"America the Beautiful" is the saying
Can it also be called this because of you?

You walk with magnificence in the glow of the sun
You glide on the beams of the silver moon
You have helped take the nation to the stars
Where it shines ever so brightly

Respectful I am of your confidence
Amazed I am of your resolve

Women across the world look at your achievements
And they dream great too

Dear Lady,
Know that in your heart of hearts

The nation loves and needs you
Always and forever

LADY OF ARUBA

ABOUT THIS POEM:

In March of 2010, I went on vacation to Aruba to run a half-marathon. While there in this beautiful, exotic country, I met the H. and the C. families from The Netherlands who were so kind to me. One of the wives suggested to me that I should write a poem about Aruba. And since it is a commonwealth of The Netherlands, I should write one about it as well.

So I took her up on both ideas. While sitting outside my hotel room (the MVC Eagle Beach, room 102) the night before the race, I wrote this poem. (You will soon read the second "suggested" poem.)

Also, music played a part in this poem. I remember listening to the smooth jazz song "Aruba Nights" by Bobby Lyle over and over again while I was writing this poem in Aruba.

Lastly, this very poem appeared on the June 5, 2010 front page of "The Aruba Morning News," which is Aruba's daily newspaper. If you type in the internet link below, you will see it along with the *previous* version of this book.

Http://issuu.com/themorningnews/docs/june_5

My lovely island princess
From the country where the breeze blows exotic
And warms the soul
You do the same and more to all whom

147

Admire you
Adore you
Love you

The world comes to your door
To marvel at your kind nature
The heavens will always miss two stars
Because of your eyes

My eyes have seen your beauty
My ears have heard your melody
My heart beats with yours
My spirit is filled with praise of you
When I inhale deeply, the sea-scented air
I imagine your splendor

Tender lady,
May your heart always remain warm and loving
Just like your country

LADY OF ASIA

ABOUT THIS POEM:

I want to tell the women in **all** the countries of Asia my thoughts about them here in this poem.

In the "Lands of the Rising Sun"
There exists a "Pearl of the Orient"
That gem is you, cherished lady

For when the sun rises in the sky
It has also risen in your heart
And that sunshine within you
Has "set" upon the world
Making it a brighter place

Your grace is like a soft summer breeze
Your honor stands strong like a mountain
Your love is like a rose in full bloom

Take me with you to the stars
So I may shine with you
And your nation

My noble empress
Know that your affection is noticed by all
Feel your devotion has caught the eyes of the world
For you have captured the hearts of many

And mine as well

Ed Hendricks

LADY OF AUSTRALIA

ABOUT THIS POEM:

I want to honor the women of Australia by "giving" them this poem. I also want to confess that my fantasy vacation is to visit Australia and dive down to The Great Barrier Reef. Maybe when I am there, I can officially "give" them this poem.

From the land "Down Under"
But your presence lifts your country up
To the stars and beyond
And then back again

In a country the sun kisses
Its lips have touched yours
And your heart

Eyes near and far have imagined you
Adored you
Admired you

You have added to the wonders of Australia
With your love
Your understanding
Your very being

An aura of excitement surrounds you
And attracts the world

I will not be the last to think of you as

Love, Sex, And Romance

Enchanting . . . exciting
Many in the world have thought the same

My glorious princess of the sun
As you live and you love
Your nation will shine with greatness

LADY OF BRAZIL

ABOUT THIS POEM:

In the "About This Poem" section of the poem "Of Love and Dreams," I "gave" my friend Talma Xavier of Recife, Brazil that poem. Now I want to "give" this poem to the women of Brazil.

In a country of sand and sun
There exists a vision of wonder
That grand sight is you, lovely lady

Inspired from the limitless mind of God
Your infinite loving heart has made your nation great

Exciting to the senses you are
For many fantasies and dreams about you
Have become reality for all to see
And cherish

You have fired up the world's imagination
Because you radiate and attract
Deep feelings of passion and romance

My precious princess
May the glory of the sun
Always shine upon your country
And your heart also

EASTERN LADY

ABOUT THIS POEM:

I want to send this poem out to the women of **all** the Middle East countries. Know that you are thought of in high regard as well.

My brave Eastern lady
In the lands where the sun shines so bright
And so do you

With a heart full of love
And a soul full of faith
Precious you are to the world
And your nations

Deep is the respect you have earned
For your devotion and sincerity are inspirations
So great your life challenges have been
And still are

One can gaze up at the stars
And imagine your eyes

Sweet lady,
Feel that God cherishes you
And he keeps your spirit close to his own
For your caring and loving nature lights his eyes up

And makes his heart glad

Ed Hendricks

LADY OF FRANCE

ABOUT THIS POEM:

The city of Paris is considered the most romantic city on Earth.
And it is the women in France that help to make it so. Because
of this fact is why I wrote this poem to them. Also, I wanted to
try something different and make this into an acrostic poem.

L oving, grand and so very
A ttractive you are, my
D arling. The world
Y earns to romance you for we have

O bserved how you have bravely and
F aithfully helped make your nation great.

F eelings of
R espect and everlasting
A dmiration of your passionate
N ature have totally
C aptured the
E ssence of who you are

LADY OF INDIA

ABOUT THIS POEM:

The women of India have helped India rise to stand out in the world. I wish to give them praise here in this poem.

From a realm of myth and mystery
Comes the brave Lady of India
For your beauty is no myth
Your charm is no mystery
They are now a reality
These traits make you more beloved
And desired

Stories of your nation's heroes should include you
Because you have won over many hearts
With your loving spirit

A treasure for the ages you are
For you are worth more than gold
More precious than silver
You shine more than a polished diamond
In the glory of the sun

Grand Lady,

Know that you have been exalted
To the celestial kingdoms
And in the paradise of eternity
Is where you will always be

Ed Hendricks

LADY OF THE NETHERLANDS

ABOUT THIS POEM:

Earlier in the "About This Poem" section of the poem "Lady of Aruba," I told you how it was suggested to me to write not only that poem, but to also write a poem to the women of The Netherlands. Here is that second poem.

My precious lady of The Netherlands
In a country that lies so low
But your heart makes it rise to the sky
And your love takes it to the stars

Such a delight it is
To know your fascinating personality
To feel your romance
To gaze into your loving eyes
And imagine eternity

The angels gaze down on you
And sing praises of your grand spirit
Their majestic melody awakens the ears of God
And he smiles with joy

Noble lady,
You have touched hearts and minds worldwide
And in heaven as well

156

LADY OF RUSSIA

ABOUT THIS POEM:

This poem is for the women of Russia. Know that you are thought of with respect and high regards too, despite recent political disagreements.

My darling lady of Russia
Delightful lady
Tender lady

With a heart as deep as infinity
And a soul that stretches across eternity

At times, your climate is cold
But your heart is warm
The flames of your love light up your country
A fiery glow the world can see and feel

Your spirit inspires your nation
And together with your love
The world shines

The eyes of the universe are upon you
For your majesty radiates like the sunshine
And sparkles like the stars

When one gazes upon you
We see a captivating lady
Charming lady

Ed Hendricks

Sensual lady

You have aroused my imagination to tell all
Just how sensational of a lady you are

SPANISH LADY

ABOUT THIS POEM:

The women of *all* the Spanish-speaking countries of the world
are to be highly prized. This poem lets them know their value.

Exquisite Spanish Lady
With eyes as beautiful as the sunrise
And hair softer than a thousand feathers

Come to me, beloved maiden
So I may adore centuries of passion in motion

Was God thinking of the stars when he imagined you?
So much about you takes breaths away
For you have won over minds and hearts worldwide

My adoring lady with your deep loving heart
A heart that is as deep as the ocean
And wider than the sea
Know that I respect your heritage
I admire your courage

The lady and the woman that you are
Amazing, fascinating
Dear Spanish lady

Ed Hendricks

LADY OF UKRAINE

ABOUT THIS POEM:

In the "Dedication" section of this book, I thanked Karina Goncharova of Kharkiv, Ukraine for letting me use her picture of the two lovers on the cover. In this poem, I want to honor her, as well as all the women of her country.

Dearest lady of Ukraine
Such a sweetheart you are
With your pleasing nature
And your joyful spirit

Your country's flag colors are blue and yellow
Blue, for your soul is deeper than the sky
Yellow, for your heart shines like the sun

Through your eyes the world can see eternity
And feel its depths there too

One can sing with the angels
And smile with God
Just thinking of you

Passionate lady,
Excited the world has become
To know you
And to love you

Love, Sex, And Romance

CONCLUSION

I would like to thank all of you dear readers for coming with me on this wonderful journey of the heart. We have gone to the stars together. We have explored space and time and the future together. We have experienced the beauty of nature and the beauty in our hearts and souls together. And it's all because of love.

In closing, I leave you with these powerful words from the Bible. I feel these great words tell the whole story of what love should be.

"Love is patient and kind; it is not jealous or proud. Love is not ill mannered or selfish or mean; love does not keep a record of wrongs. Love is not happy with evil, but is happy with the truth. Love never gives up; and its faith, hope, and patience never fails."

1 Corinthians 13: verses 4-7

Thank you all, and again, I wish you the best of life and love.

As I mentioned earlier, stay "tuned" for my next book titled "Knights of Brave Love: The Courageous Quest for Her Eternal Heart." Poems from this book will tie in with that book. You will read a fantastic "play post" (PLAY, POem, and STory combined) that spans God, time, and love. It also includes legions of warrior angels, a God empowered battle queen and the "knights" who took an oath to protect her heart, fighting against the dark forces of Hell in a titanic struggle between good against evil, and love versus hate.

For copies of this extraordinary book, or to contact me, please send an email to: Lsrthebook@gmail.com

Visit the Love, Sex, and Romance web site at:
www.Lsrthebook.com

Facebook page for Love, Sex, and Romance:
www.Facebook.com/Lsrthebook

www.ingramcontent.com/pod-product-compliance
Lightning Source LLC
Chambersburg PA
CBHW060250050426

42448CB00009B/1607